Good Morning MORNING HOLY SPIRIT

JACKI LONDON

Published By:
Jasher Press & Co.
www.jasherpress.com
customerservice@jasherpress.com
1.888.220.2068

Copyright© 2015
Interior Text Design by Pamela S. Almore
Cover Design by Pamela S. Almore
ISBN: **978-0692332863**

First Edition
Printed and bound in the United States of America

Good Morning

Morning

Holy Spirit

Jacki London

DEDICATION

I would be remised not to give honor to Apostle Billy Jacobs for my spiritual reformation in the Gospel of Jesus Christ. Twenty nine years ago, he made an impartation in me, which served as a catalyst that would catapult me into a life changing journey. From then until now, I will forever be grateful that God used him as a vessel, who would later springboard me into the birthing of this publishing,

"Good Morning, Holy Spirit"

I salute you as my Spiritual Father and Pastor. Kingdom blessings be unto you.

Table of Contents

"RISE UP, IN THE NAME OF THE LORD!"

"In the beginning was the Word, and the Word was with God, and the Word was God..."

T oday's newspapers record a state of affairs that would have been absolutely unthinkable to an observer in the 20's, 30's, 50's, etc. In the 21st Century, in which we now live, we commonly converse of how the word has been transformed into a "global village." Jet planes, instantaneous telecommunication, and integrated world of economics, and social networking sites have changed our world. Multinational corporations and conglomerates now dominate virtually every field. Yet paradoxically, we are increasingly subdividing and fragmenting along old religious lines. While the world economy becomes ever more interconnected, our relationship with God, through His Son, Jesus Christ, to be

9

non-existent on a global level. Unless human relationship can be channeled differently, this world that we live in will become Ichabod or a word without God's presence. This will definitely lead to self-destructive. I believe humanity is seeking an identity that reaches beyond the age of globalism, the quest to find "that" relationship, which fulfills the void of life, has risen among "people of the world."

I love the epistle of John. Reason being is that it is very simply, but very profound. It is unlike the synoptic gospels, which talk about the historical context of Jesus. John does not begin with the genealogy of Jesus, but with a discourse on the pre-existent Word of God and the incarnation of the Father. John removes Jesus from the realm of a prophet and shelves Him in the arena of Deity or the Godhead; giving him Homousian status, as the Father. As I exegete the scripture, I interpret that He is the Christ! He is Lord of Lord and King of Kings! He is our Risen Lord ~ the strong tower that the righteous run in and are safe! (God, I feel the Holy Ghost) He is our reigning authority in earth and heaven. His government has no end. Although the world may be experiencing the looming crisis due to an age of globalism; however the saints of God have risen above the things of this world and have entered into a "new day."

A favored day, where we will lay hands on the sick and they shall recover. A day we will live in houses that we cannot afford, drink from wells that we did not dig, and drive cars that are not in our economical means. There will come a day when vinedresser will dress our vines. The Lord is releasing the favor of the Lord and it shall dwell in your household. No longer will we be held back because of the "things" of this world.

The Lord is our Shepherd and He maketh us to lie down in green pastures... He prepares a table for us in the midst of our enemies. He is the armor of light and has set our feet in a high place~ in a wealthy place. All things were made by Him and we must remember when we dialogue in reference to the "cares of this world." He is our light and salvation, whom shall we fear. The Lord is the strength of our lives.

As John continues… Jesus says, "I am the way, the truth, and the life." God is not one dimensional, but He is a polysemantic ~ He can reach us on any and every level. All things are possible to those who believe. Whatever, the level of your faith is the level Jesus will meet you.

To some reading this literature has already sent a death certificate to your hard place. You may think you have to live with the struggles that seem so overwhelming. Maybe, you have come to a settled conclusion that "this struggle I will have to live with." But God is destroying the yoke of the oppressor and delivering you from the hand of the enemy! Although, you have engaged in a serious warfare, God will never leave you nor forsake you. He has assigned angels to war in the spirit realm for you.

This day, on your behalf, I denounce every demonic force that is coming against you from the underworld and the six regions of the earth. I denounce every diabolic and satanic force that will not allow you to see Jesus for who He is. From this day you shall encounter the power and demonstration of the Holy Spirit working and moving in your life. For He is the Alpha and Omega. The Lord is mighty in battle and is delivering you from the contacts and tactics of the enemy. Stand strong in the power of God's might, so that you can fight against the wiles of the enemy!

No matter what the enemy says, regarding the current affairs of this world… you may be in the world, but you are not of the world! And as God transfers His kingdom power to you, you are blessed because God says you are blessed! "Not by power, not by might, but by His Spirit," saith God.

DON'T DIE IN YOUR WINTER

S itting at my desk preparing for a preaching engagement tonight in my hometown. It's about 2:35a.m. I am just realizing that "a man is without honor in his own country." The battle that I am currently in is serious, beyond serious! Then at this moment of warring, I remember that I am coordinating a serious "move of God" on the east coast on Saturday at 6:00 a.m. – where intercessors, prayer warriors, and watchman on the wall will gather at Pillar of Fire Worship Center for a four hour pray meeting: "Show Me Your Glory!" The devil is horrified, but God is being glorified.

It took me years to understand the strategy of the enemy. I learned the hard way, whenever you plan to impact the Kingdom of God, the enemy will use your mind as a battlefield. He will use your spouse to discourage you. He will deplete your finances and your children will become destructive. He does anything to make you lose focus, but because we know this – we should know how to better be fierce in his kingdom.

In the midst of everything the enemy is trying to destroy~ God is faithful and will send a word to destroy the works of darkness. It is important that we always remember "out of a hard place," God will birth a Word of emancipation for His people. This allows me to know the fight is not about me or you…it is about the Kingdom of God.

As I sat here, the Lord spoke to me and said, "Don't die in your winter!" It was then I learned; a leader will never pack up in the midst of the battle. He or she will wait until the battle is over and then take flight! This made me realize it is imperative to conceptualize the power that is at our disposal in effort to comprehend the degree of success, prosperity, and victory available to us when we encounter spiritual opposition. It is good for us to pursue these Kingdom principles. The scripture, Matthew 16:19 leaped in my spirit. God has given us authority to bring systems of this world an in our personal lives, to divinely align them with what the Word is saying.

We are in a time zone where we are synchronizing with God, the Almighty and Prince of Peace! Allow me to share this with you, let's differentiate: Your "Priestly" anointing empowers you to worship and offer sacrifices of the praise to God, but it is your "Kingly" anointing that gives you power and authority to legislate, regulate, enforce, and establish- in order to reign, rule, and dominate over those dark places in your life, your region, your home, your business, your ministry, and your place of employment; you need a Kingly anointing. So when we are in intensified warfare, we need to allow the "King" within us to exercise the governmental authority of God.

In Samuel 17:46-51, David address his enemy with conviction and authority – we must do the same. In light of all that has been said, I speak over my life, your life, and our children's life these words of power:

"I decree and declare that we are unstoppable, unmovable, and unbreakable. There is nothing that the enemy can do about it! It does not matter what we are confronted with, how difficult the hard place is, our current situation may not be comfortable, the valley we are in... you are in... We are unstoppable, unmovable, and unbreakable!!! I speak a word of the Lord over our lives and let it be established this day:

"Everything in our lives is coming into alignment with the power of God RIGHT NOW In Jesus name!!"

THE POSITION AND POSTURE OF GOD'S PEOPLE

As we enter into the age of the "Apostolic Reformation," it is time for an Apostolic people to take on the spirit of Issachar. We must do so in effort to discern properly "the now." The shifting that is taking place in our spirits is designed to bring a higher level of understanding. As a result of the Body of Christ receiving a higher level of understanding, we will better be in 'sync' with the motion of the Spirit, while we are in the earth realm. Also, if we are going to better wage warfare against diabolic forces that have entered the earth through cyberspace, electronic devices, and other forms of unrighteous entertainment, we must strategically come in a corporate position under the presence of Almighty God.

We must realize that the enemy has used these tactics as an entry point to destroy our purpose, our destiny, our families, our educational system, our government, our businesses, our churches – and the list is perpetual. Until, we, as a five-fold embodiment come to where Zion is calling us; the kingdom of darkness will never be destroyed. If we are to first "bind the strong man," it is imperative that we first be encountered with a supernatural visitation from the throne room.

Upon this visitation, we must know not only how to channel but release the authority and power given to accomplish the assignment of "entering the strong man's house." We must have the Spirit of Issachar to know the "whens" and His divine visitation (to be empowered) that will enable us to put the broken pieces of our society, families, businesses, finances, minds, souls, spirits, etc. back together. It takes the anointing to destroy the yoke.

We, as the Apostolic people, are responsible for setting the spiritual climate for this universe. When the climate is set, we will go the enemy's territory and effectively serve notice to inform him that we will no longer allow him to use his devices and tactics to dominate our personage nor property. God has given us the boldness to do what we have been assigned to do and that is to tear his kingdom down!

Two things I would like to share with God's Apostolic people: 1) God is not only positioning us in this season, but He is bringing us to a place of posture. Posture that consists of righteousness and holiness. He is gathering His holy assembly and bringing us in a place that His lips are on our ears. He is speaking volume to us and we must be postured before Him astutely to receive. The Lord is speaking profoundly!

Also, we must be in a "righteous" posture that we can grab what He is saying, by the Spirit, in effort to operate in a timely manner – we are being synchronized. "Let those who have an ear, hear what the Spirit of the Lord is saying!" And when we hear what God is saying...let us move in that direction, let us follow the "cloud." 2) I am doing a series of teaching on "Righteousness" (sounds elementary, but is very much needed) in our bible study. Three of the subtopics are: Integrity (honesty); Accountability (being responsible), and Character (who you are).

It is my 'feel' that the Body of Christ needs to be re-educated on these basic foundational principals in effort to know the importance of their spiritual formation. You may have hermeneutics, but do you have integrity? You may prophecy with precision but what about your character? A gift will make room for you but your character will keep you there. You may be profound but are you accountable for your actions?

May the blessings of the Lord overtake you this day. While the blessings overtake you, taste and see that the Lord is real good!!

"For a small moment have I forsaken thee; but with great mercies will I gather thee. In a little wrath I hid my face from thee for a moment; but with everlasting kindness will I have mercy on thee, saith the Lord they Redeemer...for the mountains shall depart, and the hills be removed: but my kindness shall not depart from thee, neither shall the covenant of my peace be removed, saith the Lord that hath mercy on thee...And all they children shall be taught of the Lord; and great shall be the peace...No weapon that is formed against thee shall prosper, and every tongue that shall rise against thee to judgment thou shall condemn..."

Isaiah 54:7-8, 10, 13-14, 17

WE ARE THE RIGHTEOUSNESS OF GOD...

The 54th Chapter of Isaiah, clearly explains that God has great treasures for the righteous; the righteousness of His grace. If we, as the righteous, review our former troubles in life, it is interesting to know that God favors the righteous – His people.

Isaiah depicts Israel as a woman forsaken, as though she was a wife of youth, she had been rejected and full of discontentment. Sure you can relate to her feelings because you too have been rejected. But have you ever felt forsaken or been rejected by God? Even though we are married to God and many are 'sold out' to God, sometimes we may seem to be forsaken by God. But God's mercy always seems to prevail. Often times God will hide Himself from us just to see how we will respond to adversities when we can't trace or track Him. God is still a "good God on a bad day!"

Mountains have moved, earthquakes have shaken some of the strongest foundations – but the promises of God to the righteous have never and will never be broken by the devastation of any event. When our friends fail us – our God does not, nor does His kindness part, nor does His mercy. He will be there even until the end of time.

When everybody leaves you, God will stand with you and for you. God's kindness will never leave the righteous. For who He loves, He loves to the very end. Therefore, the covenant is re-instituted..."I will be your God and you shall be my people." God's mercy endureth throughout all generations.

Righteousness and holiness are the beauty of the church. God is interested in restoring purity, righteousness, and honesty to the church. These are the elements which bring strength and stability to any church. God is ushering spiritual mothers and spiritual fathers who have been encrypted with righteousness in order to realign the church that it will be without spot or wrinkle. God is lifting up a standard in the church – the beauty of holiness and righteousness. This remnant of people who are called by the name of God are not just looking for material attributes, lucrative lifestyles, or academic standards, but God is raising a new nation of people who are "thirsty and hungry for righteousness!" Be ye filled with the power of the Holy Ghost!

As long as there is a devil in hell there will be frequent alarms but God will own none of them. The glory of God stands between us and these frequent alarms. The day that the ungodly thinks he can come against the righteous to think he is doing God a favor, in a matter of time, their attempt will end in their own ruin. God's grace is toward the righteous.

He is a protector and a divine shield. When the evil dig a ditch for the righteous to fall in, when he builds gallops for the righteous to hang from, let him dig two because he who digs a ditch and builds the gallops for God's righteous just might be bringing demise to himself. Troubles will be troubles, distractions will be distractions, and weapons will form, but they will not be strong enough to complete the assignment against the righteous. It shall return in the face of those who use it against God's people.

When the weapons of war do not prosper, when the dirty deeds of men are non-effective, there are tongues that will rise in judgment. This is what happened when Haman came against the Jews and Mordecai, God reversed the curse. God is reversing the curse to overturn your captivity. When the wicked bring false accusations against you or try to assassin your character or maybe blemish your integrity and/or make you odious to the people and obnoxious to those in high places, God will silence them. Threatening tongues will be put to silence by well-doing. All of us who are the righteousness of God will stand in the power of God's might! When we boldly stand, God's promises will stand with us because they are the heritage of the righteous.

Yes, there are times it seems as though the enemy is gaining. Job asked a question (21:7), "Wherefore do the wicked live, become old, yea, and are mighty in power?" It always seems as though the wicked prosper in height, not only do they live, but they seem to prosper. They live and are suddenly "cut off" by God's divine stroke of destruction. They are mighty in power and are given to places of authority and trust. But in the end their prosperity and authority ripens them for their own ruin. The Bible says, "The prosperity of fools destroys them." This happened by the hardening of sin within them. They think they can live without God; therefore, they find no need to serve Him. They fail to realize that it is God who centers us and establishes us. "In Him we live, move, and have our being!" They just remember it is not in their might or in the power of their hand that they have received their wealth. Because of this, they ought to remember it is God who gave it to them...nor can they keep it without God. "The earth is the Lord's and the fullness thereof."

The wicked will not be healed by the grace of God. They are always like the sea in a storm – never finding rest. They are always guilty and full of wrath. There is no reconciliation to God for them while they continue in their trespasses and trying to plot against the righteous – the righteous create peace for those who have made Jehovah Christos their God. He will be a strong tower to them, He will cover them with his glory, and He will hide them in His pavilion and bosom. He will comfort them, heal them, and give them rest in a hard place.

When you walk in righteousness, Colossians 2:15, will minister to you. "God disarmed the principalities and powers ranged against us and made a bold display and public example of them, in triumphing over them in Him and in it [the cross]." To look at this scripture: God has taken all Satan's weapons away from him and will never return them. Jesus destroyed Satan's weapons of sin, sickness, fear, death, depression, poverty, and so forth; these arrows can no longer penetrate and are non-effective in our lives. These weapons have been rendered powerless; if Jesus found a reason to return them Satan, which I strongly doubt (why would He); they would not work against us. "For this purpose the Son of God was manifested that he might destroy the works of the devil." (John 3:8)

Jesus has destroyed the works of Satan. Satan is ruler of this world and still the prince of power of the air, there is still a spiritual battle, which Paul calls "wrestling" – for we are not wrestling with flesh and blood – contending only with physical opponents – it's not your spouse, it's not your manager, it's not your child, however it is a spirit of Satan operating through human vehicles to destroy the plan of God for your life.

It is diabolic influences, master spirits, and darkness loosed from the underworld on an assignment for Satan. You cannot fight a spiritual battle with a natural weapon, you must use the Word of God accommodated with praying in the Spirit. These shall serve as your weapons against satanic attacks. Some would ask, "If Jesus effectively rendered Satan powerless, why would we have to resist him?" Ephesians 6 advises us to put on the spiritual armor to "stand against the wiles of the devil."

Satan has many tricks, falsified information, delusions, deceptions and gimmicks that look right and/or feel right. When you pray, it is imperative that you ask God to impart in your spirit a supernatural discernment as well as His wisdom. It is necessary that you become wise to the tricks of Satan. He has reached back into his satanic power machine and in his presentation to equate with what appears good.

The scripture says, "Shun the very appearance of evil." The only way he has authority over us is that we submit and agree to his wiles. When we talk negative, we submit and agree to his wiles, when we complain; we submit and agree to his wiles. The tongue is powerful, so be careful how you use it. His strategy is to make us believe he still has effective weapons and can manifest to us what he is threatening us with.

The Bible declares not only is Satan is a liar but he is the father of all lies!!!

The reason we still have problems in certain areas of our lives such as poverty, sickness, divorce, fear, addiction, etc. is because we believe and receive what Satan says about our situation more than we believe what the "Word" says about our situation. Often times we will say the "Word" of God is true, but will not act on it because it is easier to believe a lie (Satan) than believe the truth (God). The truth of the matter is; we must, absolutely must, find scriptures in reference to our situation to enforce and apply those scriptures to our problems.

The scripture gives life – the scripture is oxidated, it is a living organism. Why speak death over your marriage when you can speak life over your marriage? Why speak death over your finances when you can release the power of life into your bank account? God sent His word and healed us from every problem that we may be confronted with. David said, "I sought the Lord and He heard me and delivered me from all my fears!" Not only did God hear you, but He delivered you from all your fears! Oh God!!!

You have the victory, you are an ambassador and you are not just a conqueror, you are more than a conqueror in Jesus Christ. You shall live and not die to proclaim the works and the Word of the Lord!! This type of victory has been manifested in the spirit realm. So in order to receive this authority, you must grab it by the spirit – it's a spiritual "thing!" You must hear, not with your natural ear but with your spirit, what the Lord is saying. This is not by flesh and blood, but this is by the Spirit of the True and Living God! You have victory over sin, you have victory over fear, you have victory over your flesh, you have victory over your mind, and you have the victory over adverse situations in your home, in your business, on your job...you have the victory through Jesus Christ.

As children of righteousness, as Spirit Filled Believers, we must know the purpose, the ability of the dominion power, and the Kingdom of the Lord is within us. We must, at all times, operate out of this supernatural power and authority given to declare, demand, and decree that we are no longer bound by the influences of this world nor the strongholds of Satan. God is severing the soul ties that have bound us to Satan.

Jesus said, "...how can one enter the strong man's house, and spoil his goods, except he first bind the strong man and then he will spoil the house. (Matthew 12:29) God has given us the dominion power and legal right to dominate and rule in the earth realm. Rise up in your spirit to receive what God is doing in this Apostolic hour. It is our task to keep Satan defeated and controlled so that his wiles will never be effective on this earth. When we remind him that "it is written," according to God's Word, he must bow his knees to God's will in every situation. I suggest that you take a dominant stance against whatever is in your life you know is out of the will of God – take a dominant stance against those things that do not line up with the Word of God – do it right now! Close the door in Satan's presence and tell him..."you do not live here anymore!!!"

Never live beneath your rights as a "Son of God" – you not only have the victory but you are triumphed in Jesus Christ. To distinguish the two: victory is when one opponent wins the battle over the other – the loser surrenders to the winner, the contest is terminated and the loser agrees to abide by the rules of the winner. Triumphing is what follows the victory. For example, when the 4th of July came, we as citizens of the USA celebrated our independence from the English regime.

We don't have to fight the war again because the war is over. Since we won, we have the right to celebrate our triumph because of that victory. When Jesus died on the cross and rose from the dead, He won the victory over Satan. He does not have to return to the cross and be raised from the dead every time we face a hard place. Those things have been nailed to the cross. That was has been completed. So we don't have to go through life fighting a battle of fear, sin, poverty, depression and so forth because Jesus has already fought and won that battle for us. Do you believe?? If you do, celebrate or triumph over Satan every day because you know the Truth. Clap your hands and open your mouth ... release a shout of praise unto your God! "Thanks be unto God, which always causeth us to triumph in Christ." (2Corinthians 2:14) Through the death of and resurrection of Jesus Christ, Satan no longer has authority over your situation. God has disarmed him. Satan can only step to you "as a roaring lion!"

Today, as the Righteousness of God, you can triumph in and through Jesus Christ. You are no longer defeated. From this day forth, you no longer have to stand on the sidelines hoping Jesus does not pass you by to be released from a situation, or to overturn your captivity, or to undo your heavy burdens, or to break the yoke of bondage operating in your life. Let this be imparted in your spirit – speak deliverance to your soul and walk out of fear, walk out of brokenness, walk out of poverty, and walk out of that sickness – through the Word of God. You can now enjoy the spoils from the strongman's house – prophesy to yourself and demand, declare, and decree that the hard place(s) in your life has been broken and destroyed. The anointing destroys the yoke. Loose God's presence in your situation and speak life. Loose God's presence in your situation and speak life over what Satan has pronounced dead. There is resurrecting power in the name of Jesus! As I speak these words of power through this message, the blood of Jesus is prevailing in your situation to free you from a place of restriction – rejoice as a child of righteousness and be glad in the God of your salvation! Affirm that another war has been won! Do you believe??

Stand in righteousness, my sister and my brother – for your righteousness has come up before the Lord

God Almighty and His glory rest between you and the unrighteous!

You are blessed and highly favored of the Lord!

THE NEW "NEXT"...

Before the break of dawn is when God normally puts His lips to my ears to say, "In this season expect to drink new wine!" As I began to get the revelation if He's going to change our lives to new wine, we must be living or drinking old wine. The contrast is the old and the new. We cannot pour new wine into old wineskins. In the Jewish culture, wine was very well processed and in the last stages, carbon dioxide generated by the fermentation process would stretch the wineskins to its limit causing the wineskin to rupture and the new wine to gush out and be wasted. Job says it so well: "For I am full of matter, the spirit within me constraineth me, Behold my belly is as wine which hath no vent; it is ready to burst like new bottles." (Job 32:18-19)

There is a breaking forth in you and for you. The "new you" cannot live in an old place. You cannot join old to the new; you will ruin both the new wine and the old skin. You are feeling uncomfortable in an old place because the atmosphere of an old place is too small for you to reside. Therefore, we must expect to live in a new state of existence.

Strangely enough, the pressures of life have shifted us into this "new" life. It is a Job theology, "I am so full I am ready to burst like new bottles." Isaiah says, "Old barren women, sing a new son!" We are being regenerated with new wine. The Jews way of thinking was, "Old is better than new." They felt it better because they were comfortable with the old way. Sometimes we get complacent in an old state of being because it is easier dealing with the old place of employment, the old community, the old relationship, and the old traditional Church, even an old government as in religion…it's easier, it's more comfortable, it's a familiar place. But God says you cannot pour new wine into old wineskins – you'll ruin both.

Today, God is calling us out of our comfort zone. Launch out! Our state of existence is changing, climb after climb; we are on our way to a better day – new wine! As we shift, let's not drag old things into new lives. For the Lord Himself shall "turn our water into new wine!

GOD, SHOW ME YOUR GLORY!

Isn't God awesome! His glory validates and sanctions us as the "Sons of God." Also, the cloud of God's glory and presence show His approval. In Exodus 33:12-16 the scripture says"...my presence shall go with thee and I will give thee rest." It is His glory that rest upon us when we are confronted with oppositions or when adversities seem to loom the thresholds of our tomorrows. His glory serves as a self-sustaining power. There is nothing that can compare or equate to the mystical power and glory of the Holy Spirit. God reveals Himself to Moses through the glory cloud and begins to speak, "Behold, I make a covenant before all the people. I will do marvels, such as have not been done in all the earth, or in any nation: and all the people among which thou shall see the work of the Lord: for it is a great thing that I will do with thee." Saints of God, it is so imperative that we stay under the shadow of the Almighty, which is His presence. Everything flows from the presence of God; troubles vanish, hearts are mended, minds are delivered, bodies are healed, and lives are changed while in the presence of God. God's power is what He does but His presence is who He is. You cannot have a divine encounter with God through His glory and remain the same. God not only transforms us, but He transfigures us to become "eyewitnesses of his majesty."

In Matthew 17:1-8, Peter cites, "Lord, it is good for us to be here..." What was Peter witnessing on the mountain top? He was witnessing a display of God's full reign as His son, Jesus Christ. Through the transfiguration of Jesus or changed form of Jesus, the gospel writer speaks of his face becoming bright like the sun, and of His clothes dazzling white, whiter than we can imagine. In Exodus, Moses dialogues with requesting "let me see your glory." God honors his request by saying, "I can't let you see my glory, but when I pass by you, you will know that my glory has prevailed!" He further told Moses that, "there is a place in the cleft of the rock that you may sit next to me."

On this day, there is a witness in my spirit that God's presence is passing by us not only to transform us or change our inner character, but He wants to transfigure us through the glory cloud that is overshadowing our very lives in this moment. He wants to reveal to us that He is God's chosen one. There is divine connection and a covenant agreement declared by God Himself to Born Again Believers. No matter what Satan says or tries to form against us, the glory of God shall stand up in an unprecedented, unexplainable way to declare that the glory of God does not only walk with us, but lives inside of us.

God's dominion power is within us and if you believe in this as the scripture says, "out of your belly, will flow rivers of living water, rivers of power, rivers of an anointing, rivers of authority, rivers of liquid fire, and rivers of His glory!" There will be no demonic activity that can defy the works, the purpose, or the destiny that God has given us or called us into. No man shall be able to stand against you because this day forth you stand under the glory cloud of the Most High God. He reigns and super rules in your life, in your seed's life, in your marriage, in your finances, in your business, on your job, and in your home. God has sanctioned you and validated you to be transfigured that you may operate on a higher level. Through the power of the Holy Ghost, God snatches you out of where you are and takes you to the third heaven (what a pivotal moment!!! Glory to God!!)

The Lord makes an impartation of His glory within you to divinely and richly connect you with heaven that demons, warlords, witches from or the underworld are denounced from your presence.

"This is that," Peter talks about it ~ "It is good that I be here." Where is "here?" That place where you no longer look like sin, but you look like God's glory. "Here" is where the flavor of favor is prevalent and is manifested and demonstrated through your life that every place the sole of your feet tread is not only blessed but belongs to you. "Here" is where you break your alabaster box to say, "Not my will but your will be done in my life." "Here" is where your very shadow released the supernatural flow of these things to mark you as a signet of the true and living God!!!

About right now, you should feel the power, the presence and the fire of the Holy Ghost turning an churning on the inside of you in effort that He works a new work in you and through you that Hell cannot suppress!!

THERE IS MORE TO YOUR LIFE
THAN ITS PRESENT STATE

The master plan that God has for you is unconditional. Your footsteps to this place in life have been ordered by the Lord. What an explosive time… life is now taking a road of its own through the Holy Spirit and God is beginning to do some things out of order and out of sequence. Things are getting ready to take an unexpected turn… He is turning some things over, and shaking some bushes just for you, His beloved. Honestly speaking, it has nothing to do with you, but the people you will meet in the next six months. There is a testimony that God will allow to come forth out your Spirit-man like rivers of living water. A testimony that will make a deposit in someone else's life to assure them that "Jesus is real!" A testimony that will cause people to live and not die. Through your trials and tribulation, God has given you the signet ring and coat of many colors as a proven fact that heaven has documented and the Holy Spirit of God has validated you as a first class citizen in the category of "THESE ARE THEY!" The tribulations have been great, but you are an overcomer! The power of God is moving in your favor to bring forth a divine connection, a divine intervention, and divine favor. "And ye shall be my people and I will be your God."

Now is the hour that bridges you to forgotten unanswered prayers; prayers that you have stored in your secret closest and left on the shelf. Miraculous testimonies shall come forth. The mighty hand of God reaches on those dusted shelves to bring to pass utterances that seemed impossible. The atmosphere has been made conducive to receive the release from the spirit realm to the earth realm.

God is transferring His power from the throne room to you in effort that it may empower and impact you to operate out of a higher level. Also, to receive the manifestation and demonstration of the unfolding mystery that your deepest desires are hinged upon. He gets the glory; go tell someone else of His goodness and mercy and how He brought you out. It is good that you are in this place! This place is a place of brokenness. This is a place of being "sold out," a place where He has pitched a tent for you and built an ark. Sojourn in this place. This place is a place of "if I perish, let me perish, but I'm going to see the King!

I feel a "nevertheless" anointing coming upon somebody who is reading this writing. You know why I feel a "nevertheless" anointing? Well let me tell you; somebody who has been going through hell for the last ten years, is getting a "breakthrough," somebody had to live with demons for the most part of their life is getting a "breakthrough," somebody that's been "dogged" out and don't know what to do is getting a "breakthrough." When "nevertheless" hits the atmosphere you can't help, but to break free – it's the anointing that destroys the yoke!

The anointing is operating in the atmosphere. Excuse me, I'm receiving a fax from God, it says… "Quickly, submerge yourself under Rauch and do not operate outside the elements of the Holy Spirit." When the anointing hits the atmosphere it comes to take resident in two ways: 1) to gird you up; and 2) to speak!

As you read, the anointing is speaking to your spirit –
"I'm hearing, delayed doesn't mean denied, you are in
sync with Me, this is your appointed time." Can I tell
you what the anointing is saying? The anointing is
saying "this is your third day, it is finished, and all your
prayers are being answered!" That is what the anointing
is saying. Out of your brokenness, God will require of
you to do things you've never done before to get what
you've never had before. Must I say this dispensation of
your life... the rules change. God will require, not faith
of a grain of a mustard seed, but immeasurable faith.

The bible says in Luke 12:48 that, 'For unto
whomsoever much is given, of him shall be much
required..." Your faith is being mandated. Reason being
is because you never thought this could happen for you
– you never knew God this way! Therefore you must
rise up and receive in your spirit, "Your eyes have not
seen, your ears have not heard, nor has it entered into
the heart of man what God has prepared for you!"

Listen that is not when you get to heaven, this is
now! It is taking immeasurable faith to grab what God
is doing in the earth realm; the strangeness of God is
being exposed to those who can believe immeasurably.
God is establishing a covenant in you, everything you

set out to do – the Holy Spirit is going to back you in power… "Behold, the days come, saith the Lord, that I will make a new covenant with the house of Israel, and with the house of Judah: Not according to the covenant that I made with their fathers in the day that I took them by the hand to bring them out of the land of Egypt, which my covenant they brake, although I was an husband unto them, saith the Lord, But this shall be the covenant, that I will make with the house of Israel, after those days saith the lord, I will put my law in their inward parts and write it in their hearts: and will be their God, and they shall be my people." Praise our God that sounds like good news… it is good news!

Lastly, obey God rather than man. God has the power to exalt you. Promotion does not come from the north, south, east, or west; it comes from God. Why do I interject this statement? Because the enemy will try to make deals and transactions with you to abort your miracles. In this hour he will try to deceive you through people that are assigned to bring you under the control of witchcraft (rebelliousness) – to pull you out of the spirit realm. Their way will look right and good, but they won't look "God." The bible says, "There is a way unto man that seems right, but the end shall bring forth death."

Satan will try to influence you to operate in the realm of sense and knowledge, but not so! This is a God thing, this is God's way... when the enemy comes in like a flood, let the purpose of God be released out of your mouth. God has exalted you to a place in Him in a double fold measure – to be a blessing and to receive a blessing. Don't let the trickery of the enemy move you out of position.

"My sheep know my voice and a stranger's voice they shall not hear." The Lord knoweth how to deliver the godly out of temptations, and to reserve the unjust unto the Day of Judgment to be punished. Remember, what you have gone through and what you are getting ready to be blessed with is not about you, but it is to bring glory to God's name that others may see Him in an exalted position. When you lift up the name of Jesus somebody will be delivered and saved.

This is why the enemy would want to silence you; this is why the enemy would want you to believe He is the exalted one. Now, let us not forget, the enemy does not come in a red suit with horns and a pitchfork. He operates through someone who knows your weakness and then presents an opportunity to expound in that area. Stay focused! What God is doing in you, strangely enough, is not about you, but About His glory.

That is why it is important that I say to you, "guard your spirit and protect your anointing!!" So that you can forever give God praise and glory for His wondrous works. If you do these things, the master plan of God will never cease to operate in your life, it will unfold! The unanswered and forgotten prayers will manifest and there will be a demonstration of the power of the Holy Ghost in your life. Continue fighting the good fight of faith, immeasurable faith – it is your moment!

"The thief cometh not, but for to steal, and to kill, and to destroy; I am come that they night have life, and that they might have it more abundantly." John 10:10

I believe that every one of us can testify to a moment in our lives when it seemed as though we have experienced a dreadful and deplorable moment. A moment when there was no "Word" from the Lord. We can call this an inter-testimonial period. Some of us have or are still engaging in conflicts so extensive that unless God destroys the yoke, we will be forced to live in the mediocrity mold.

In viewing the named scripture, there is a contrast between Jesus and Satan, the thief.

The thief is the personification of Satan and he has an agenda. His agenda is to present situations to us that will steal, kill, and destroy our ability to become victorious, our ability to walk in destiny, and our ability to fulfill our God given purpose. Please know that he will come in. The scripture does not say "if" but it says "when" the enemy comes in like a flood... understand with absolute certainty that hell will break loose in your life at some given time. This is not an adjunction, nor a hyperbole, nor a metaphor – it is a certainty. Continue blessing the Kingdom of God; continue giving tithes, seeds, offerings, continue being committed and loyal and you will, with certainty, experience hell's activity.

But when all hell does break loose, we have got to make sure that it is not self-inflicted. Sometimes, we can become our own enemy by making wrong decisions, have the wrong motives, listening to ungodly counsel, and failing to obey/respect leadership. Therefore, I impose the question, are you satanically induced or self-inflicted? Regardless of your answer, there is a way out. Jesus counteracts the thief's agenda and profoundly states…"I am come that they might have life and that they might have it more abundantly."

Remember Jesus and the thief will never exchange characteristics. The demarcation line is set and Jesus has set the center of your life and it will not cross over into demonic territory unless we remove our "war clothes" and give up the "ghost." Regardless to your situation(s), circumstance(s), or struggle... you cannot draw a circumference. Why? God is enlarging your territory and you are a person of abundance, you are a person of greatness, and a person of dominion power. It seems you have been in a place of obscurity, but you have reached your pivotal point. A place where God changes everything, your prayer has brought you here, your prayer has brought you "out," your prayer has brought you through, to a place of release.... released from the strongholds that are designed to kill, steal, and destroy your vision, your life, your dream, your children, your business, your finances, and your community.

Through this scripture, God has given you the authority to stand strong in the midst of the enemy. He has given you a "word" of power that you are not going to die in your struggle, but you are going to have life and life more abundantly. I encourage you to speak John 10:10 over your situation for the next ten days and just observe the demon chasing, yoke destroying power that bruises the head of the enemy. The joke, I mean the yoke (te-he-he) the enemy has placed over your life will and has become nullified - you will be able to testify through the blood of the Lamb... that God brought you out... right on time! Be blessed. God shall catapult you into the volume of the book that is written about you!

God has not forgotten you. In this explosive season, God shall remember His people in a great way. I am led to send this "Word" to you because I hear the cry of God's people in my spirit. This cry is leading me to believe that your soul has melted because of life's storms. You have fainted and have come your "wits end!" Can I give you a word of advice? In the midst of the stormy wind, do not jump off the ship, but readjust your sail. God is calming the storm, so that the waves and wind are still. Throughout my spiritual formation, I have learned that when I have prayed out of my spirit and still there is no answer for my situation, God has a bigger picture.

In instances such as these, the Bibles tell us to "stand still and see the salvation of the Lord!" During this inter-testimonial period when life seems deplorable because there is no theophy or no prophetic voice, the enemy would love to get the glory as a result of you moving impulsively as you compromise with him. Warning! If you move out of season, your actions will only produce an "Ishmael."

When you cannot get an answer, "don't move until God moves." When the warfare intensifies, when the problems have multiplied, when you feel that everything has gone wrong that can go wrong, when you have come to your "wits end," know that God is in the preliminary stages of changing your state of existence. Know that the laws of Heaven are being legislated into your life and God is summoning angels from heaven as demonstration of the Holy Spirit brings forth the evidence of His power in your situation. God remembers you and His Holy promise. He will bring you forth with great joy. "The people asked... and He satisfied them with the bread of heaven. He opened the rock and the waters gushed out; they ran in dry places like a river (Psalms 105:40-41)." The Holy Spirit will trouble your stagnated water. In this season, God is bringing you from "what is" to "what shall be." In the Kingdom of God there are five seasons: winter, spring, summer, fall, and the due season. God is making way for your "due season." Discerning seasons are majorly important. He has remembered you with favor – underserved access, with His grace and mercy.

THE STRUGGLE IS OVER!

Would I be spiritual correct to say this is the season that God is doing strange things, quickly? The water is troubled; angels have troubled the waters. Is there anyone out there that can bear witness to the twenty first century apostolic supernatural "move" of the Holy Spirit?

This year has proven itself to be an explosive year and the miracles upon your life are now becoming opulent. There is a shake in the house of the Lord and the very foundation of the enemy is being overturned. Now that you have suffered awhile God has settled you, strengthened you, and established you. God is doing a "twist off" in your life. God is propelling you into new things suddenly and surely.

Retribution comes to your house – which will be the reward for your faithfulness, integrity, and accountability. This retribution is being received from the land that has been stolen from your lineage, children that you lost through the prison system, through the cracks of society, through the mental institutions, through rehabilitation centers, marriages loss to addictions, employment positions that you have loss to co-workers less qualified than you, homes that were foreclosed, bank accounts loss through a failed economy, loss retirement revenues, and business gone bad... yes, retribution comes to your house! The years that the locust, palmerworm, and cankerworm has stolen from you shall be restored in this season – in the next three months.

2014 is the acceptable year of the Lord. It is a year that the sons (does not mean gender, but all inclusive) of God are to be celebrated. The Holy Spirit of God is putting some things in motion. He is taking space out of distance – what would have taken years to be birthed. He is birthing now. I feel an unction in my spirit to inform you that there will be quick turnarounds in your life. He has released the "pause" button.

In this year of establishment, the greatness of God will shine through you in an unprecedented manner. So much so, that you will change not only the atmosphere of your environment, but the atmosphere of those who are connected to you. Those who are in your nucleus will know that your very shadow is the weight of His glory and shall be made available to heal the sick, set the captive free, and preach the gospel to the poor.

It is your hour to just "show up" and your presence shall change the atmosphere. The Kingdom of God within you is the guest of honor in every occasion. And everything shall move by His power and come subject to the Holy Spirit of the True and Living God. In this season, you will serve as an agent of change and shall have means to be someone's answer. You will become employed by companies, you will buy houses in communities, and you will fellowship with churches just to change the atmosphere.

Even as God is using you to change the atmosphere of others, He will springboard you into a new lifestyle... Yes, your lifestyle shall be changed. He is positioning you for financial prosperity. (Can I insert this, please if you will allow me? Financial prosperity does not change people it just pronounces what is already in them.) Your name will be a trusted name in the community.

The enemy's assignment is to take territory and region over your life; therefore, be careful not to bargain with him or be in agreement with him. Satan's greatest desire is for you to bring your God under his subjection. The key in this season is to submerge under the Holy Spirit, obey delegated authority, and stay focused. God will lead and guide you into your changed day. As I hear the voice of God speaking to my spirit, some of you reading this book will make investments without portfolios and are uneducated in how to make investments, but that will not interfere with what God wants to do in your life.

Others will make successful business transactions in cities and states they never dwelled in, but will do so via telephone and cyberspace, while some will be forced into manager positions and have no knowledge or credentials for the position, but the eccentricity of God will show up and show off. However, many will receive night visions for marketing strategies that will enhance the Kingdom of God. Those who have an ear, hear what the Lord is saying: "I have not forgotten you, thus saith the Lord! I repent for the many things you have suffered, but now is the time I am crossing my hands for you and those who were last shall now be first.

I shall do some things that will be out of sequential order. For it shall be that I have brought thee into the land which I swore unto thy fathers, to give the great and goodly cities, which thou buildest not and houses full of all good things, which thou filled not, and wells dugged which thou duggest not, vineyards and olive trees, which thou plant not. For I have released Michael, the warring angel to war against the kingdom of the Prince of Persia – for I heard your prayers 21 days ago. Remember not the former things, for the antiquated symbols of the past shall be forgotten and I shall do a new thing and you shall that it is I – for you have come into a new season. For thou shalt be blessed above all people and your children shalt not be barren; I will cause the blessings to flow unto your inheritance and to your children's children. The wealth of the sinner shall be laid up for the just. Sojourn in this place that I have called you into, many will question your readiness, but know that I have given you promotion.

I have caused you to mount up as an eagle. Fear not, for it is I that have caused my blessings upon you to make you rich and that you feel no sorrow. In this hour, I will yoke you under my anointing and bring you under the captivity of the Holy Spirit that my joy and peace shall remain with you," saith the Lord! I say unto you, my fellow laborers in Christ assign and align yourself with God.

If not, you will have a problem rededicating your prosperity to Him. "Beware lest thou forget the Lord, which brought thee forth out of the land of Egypt and from the house of bondage." I am in total agreement with heaven about what God is doing. For years, many of us have struggled financially, in ministry, in marriage, with children, in business, and on jobs. But God is shaking the foundation of enemy. And with a shout, we can say, "the struggle is over!" The anointing is destroying the yoke of struggle and the burden shall be removed from your shoulder. The very surveillances of the enemy are being broken off your life. His signs are being frustrated and eliminated, so that they shall no longer hinder what God has purposed and destined for you from the very foundation of the earth. Do you believe, God?? Be blessed of the Lord and remember when strange things start happening in your life, you need to give God a "waving offering."

"Turn Ye" To A New Direction

Throughout the years of my spiritual formation, I have learned to not get comfortable where I was and always be ready to make a turn into where God is propelling me. There is a "third day" mantle resting into your atmosphere. This mantle has fallen upon the earth and is waiting for you to reach out and pick it up. There is a sound that this mantle is releasing in your atmosphere. This sound is that of revival and newness. This sound summons angels to marshal in heaven and legislate the laws of heaven for the Born Again Believer.

There is an apostolic alignment being ushered into the earth that is turning you from information to revelation – a place where God gives you understanding by the spirit. "No more living as usual!" This alignment brings a time of transitioning; it brings a time where everything seems out of sorts; it brings a time where everything seems uncertain. Out of sorts because you are longer in control of your life – the Holy Spirit is taking over; uncertain because you are experiencing a character of God you've never encountered.

The Holy Spirit is in charge and has proven that everything is moving by the Spirit of God! Everything is coming subject to the Spirit of God! I mean everything!! Because this is a very overwhelming time for you, you are asking – "What is my pilgrimage; where do I go from here?" The peculiarity about this transition – He may not show you how you are going to get "there," but when you look up you will find yourself in a place called "there." God is taking you out of "what is" into "what shall be."

He is taking space out of distance – let me tell the truth – it is just a day of a supernatural move of God. I feel a suddenly and a surely power surge… God is speaking volume to your life. But do not evade the imperative question you must ask yourselves, "Am I standing in the correct posture to receive this deeper dimension and higher level from God?" If you are anything like me, in this hour, you need a tangible signposts from Him, making his presence known to help you excavate your past and to uncover some "stuff" that may have hindered you; "stuff" you may have missed that could have sabotaged or is sabotaging the flow of this supernatural move.

After being able to confront these things, I have an unction in my spirit that something is in process of happening for you – in a "twinkling of an eye." This something will change your state of existence. How do you handle life when it changes abruptly? It brings to mind Barack Obama, the President of the United States of America. He goes from not being able to attend the Democratic Convention (for whatever reason), to being the Democratic Convention Acceptance Keynote Speaker, to being the candidate for the Democratic Presidential Nominee that gives his acceptance speech before 85,000 people, to the President of the United States of America.

I feel escalation, I feel God doing a catapulting twist in your life. It is as though God will cause you to go to bed one way and while you sleep, He changes your day... Right there, I feel that the anointing is resting upon your life. Your existence is getting ready to change. What do you do when you feel life is transitioning, but you just can't compartmentalize the transition?

The Israelites had been in Horeb for forty years when the Lord spoke to Moses saying, "Ye have dwelt long enough in this mount: Turn you, and take your journey...

beholds I have set the land before you: go in and possess the land which the Lord swears into your fathers… The Lord your God hath multiplied you… The Lord God of your fathers make you a thousand times so many more as He hath promised!" (Deuteronomy 1:8-11) God knows the length of time you have dwelt in one place, rather it be natural or spiritual. He takes assessment of your spirit man, while you are in a place of "nothingness." Whenever we run into stagnation, a place of complacency, or a hard place – God prepares us to make a decision that involves change; He is nonverbally communicating that we have dwelt long enough in one place. As you look at the scripture, Moses spoke unto the Israelites to let them know that the Lord had given him a commandment. He begins his narrative with their removal from Mount Horeb – "Turn ye"... Mount Horeb is symbolic to a place of stagnation and complacency.

God orders Moses to decamp from this place and proceed to a new place, a place of promise and new beginning – the land of Canaan. When God commands us to "turn" and go forward, He sets before us a place more fruitful than where we left. (Remember, when God gives us an assignment to "turn" there is no longer glory on the old place. We are to turn from and if our spirit or body remains there, it is a possibility that we turn to salt.)

Somehow in the midst of the transition, He overtakes us with His grace and enabling power to move quickly without struggle, without hindrance, and without sorrow. In this new move God, 80% of the people you thought would walk with you, be with you, celebrate you, are not ready or anointed to be partakers of the newness. When God told Moses to "Turn ye…" – many who initially started with him in Mount Horeb did not enter into the land of Canaan; they were left behind for whatever reason. Don't be like those who were left behind – receive in your spirit what God is doing "now" – release the old government and take on, submit, and receive where God wants to take you in this season. Move from Mount Horeb (an old place) and break forth on the left, and break from on the right… Sing a new song, oh barren woman, and let God do a new thing – for it shall spring forth and you shall know that it is the Lord thy God.

Let Him enlarge your territories; let him expand your borders. God spoke to Moses, "Behold, I have set the land before you; go in and possess the land which the Lord swore unto your fathers…" I can testify to the things of God and I am sure you can also – God is a God of His

Word. His Word will not return void, but it will fulfill its purpose – a promise is a promise! God is who He says He is and He will do what He says He will do. God has put a strong spirit in you to operate boldly before the throne of grace.

The Holy Spirit is operating in you – "go in" and possess that which God has for you. In your doing so, do not give up, do not give in – but operate boldly and stand on the Word of God. In the finality, I say unto you... "The Lord your God hath multiplied you, and behold, ye are this day as the stars of heaven for multitude. The Lord God of your fathers makes you a thousand times so many more as ye are, and bless you, as he hath promised you." (Deuteronomy 1:10) The blessing of the Lord maketh thee rich and adds no sorrow!

I RATHER OBEY GOD THAN MAN

God's authority is superior. His commands overrule; therefore they cannot nor should not be governed by reason or rational thinking. God rules with the power of truth and dominion. It is important to obey God and not man. He's not one dimensional. He is polysemantic. He is the way, the truth, and the life. The Holy Spirit of God will never lead us wrong. He will always lead and guide us into righteousness.

God is speaking to someone's heart who is reading this "word"; someone who is trying to justify making a sacrifice rather than being obedient to what God has instructed them to do. When God speaks differently from what is convenient or easier for us – when we find ourselves caught between a "rock and a hard place" –

when faith is just not the answer, we tend do one of the three: 1) obey flesh and take the easy road by following through according to sight 2) seek ungodly counsel and/or 3) make excuses. I must admit that obeying the voice of God is not always easy to submit under. From experience, God will instruct you to operate out of nothing, but I am witness that if you move toward His voice, He will back you in power.

In the incubation stage of ministry, obeying God's voice was very frightening. Many days, with two members, I wanted to throw in the towel. Often times the enemy will use someone who is in relationship with you to discourage you, manipulate you, sabotage the plan, and end negative influences to you in effort to talk you out of the divine plan of God for your life. That is why we have to be careful and have wisdom to know what to share with even our spouses, our family members, and our prayers intercessors.

We must know that we are predestined and have the purpose of God abiding in our lives. We must seek God to know what that purpose is. So many of us miss God because we don't know His voice with clarity; therefore, it is impossible to understand His plan for our lives. For this reason, we must seek His face and not

His hand. When we do these things, we will not be so easily influenced by negativity from those who operate out of subliminal jealousy against us. Yes, jealousy! If people are not for you... can I be honest... admit it, they are against you. Man said that I had missed God, when transitioning from prayer meetings in the home to initializing a traditional church setting. I remembered it was God who gave me instruction to initiate an organized church, not man. I had to remind myself; I had to "self-talk" myself that there is no failure in God.

A key scripture that ministered to me and always manifested in my spirit – it also brought me into agreement with heaven: - "to obey is better than sacrifice." (1 Samuel 15:22) If God said it, He will perform it. Man will give you advice, psychiatrist will give you advice, your prayer partner will give you advice, even your spouse will give you advice, but if it is doesn't come in agreement with the Holy Spirit has spoken into your spirit, it is against the will of God for your life.

Obedience is a principal that, we as Born Again Believers, must apply throughout our spiritual formation. The reason being, prosperity always follows an act of obedience. Disobedience "pulls" us out of the spirit realm and shifts us unto place of struggle and chaos. To this day, I am glad that I subjugated myself to the voice of God.

Today, the church has the heartbeat of Jesus Christ and is glorifying God's name. If you want to see the miraculous power of the Holy Spirit operating in your life continuously, move and synchronize with God's calendar, and keep your eyes in tune with God. When you follow the direction of God, He will go before you and make the crooked ways straight, bring down the high mountains, and fill up the low valleys.

His Word will be like a lamp unto our feet and a light unto our paths. You may not understand why, but just as Jesus spoke to the servants at the wedding of Canaan by telling them to fill the water pots, of course, they did not understand, but with authority Mary said, "Just do it!" Obedience ceases the midnight hours, moves mountains, breaks struggles off lives and brings you into the flow of God.

In Acts 5:29, Peter and the other apostles answered the high priest saying, "We ought to obey God rather than men." Man will try to divert you from the plan of God for your life by giving you all kind of reasons why you should not submit to the voice of the Holy Spirit.

They will convince you that the plan God has given you cannot be done; it's too expensive, you don't have the finances; that job is too hard for you, you'll never make it, or this is not the timing of the Lord. All sorts of negative influence will infiltrate your spirit man, (this is why it is important that we protect our spirit), but they will never or you should never allow them to overpower the voice of God. God's voice is a nail in a sure place.

If God said it, just do it! Don't worry yourself with how, when, and where, get in God's presence and He will give you a strategic plan and then begin speaking the word over your life − It is written, "I can do all things through Christ that strengthens me!" Follow the instruction of God; follow the voice of God, not of men. After Jesus spoke to the apostles and told them to preach and teach in His name; in Acts 5, the high priest had commanded the apostles not to teach in the name of Jesus.

He accused them of filling Jerusalem with "their" doctrine, but then there stood one in the council, a Pharisee, named Gamaliel, a doctor of the law, who had a reputation among all the people, and commanded to put the apostles forth a little space. God will always send a witness to agree with you, stand up for you, and to give you a "little space" to operate. This person may not be your spouse or your prayer warrior; it may be someone you don't even know, someone that believes in the Holy Spirit in you, someone that God has assigned to you for that season. Someone that is willing to touch and agree with you even when your vision does sound "off," and even when it seems impossible. See, we don't need to know a lot of people we just need to know and have a Gamaliel in our lives. Someone who will say, "Leave this child of God alone, for if the counsel of this work be of men, it will come to naught, but if it be of God, ye cannot overthrow it." You cannot overthrow the work of God. He is powerful. He is too mighty.

When Satan says, no God will follow through on His plan for your life. I remember some years ago, maybe as many as seven, I had a position as a Tax Collector. God had just promoted me on my job and while I was sitting at my desk, I was wondering how the next month's bills were going to be paid. Even though I had just received a promotion in pay, it still wasn't enough because exaltation does not come from man (Psalm 75:6).

76

God said, in Deuteronomy 8:17, "I give you power to get wealth." Let us admit it; we will never become prosperous or rich on man's job. As I held my head down in bondage to the demon of debt, God spoke in my spirit and this is what He said, "It is time for you to come off your job; I need you in full-time ministry. I need you as an intercessor." My response was, "WHAT! I can't even pay my bills with a job, how can I pay them without a job?" He spoke in my spirit and said, "Your job is not your source, I AM that I AM, Just do it!"

Of course my family and my co-workers thought I had lost my mind, sometimes they convinced me that I had lost my mind. They even gave good reason why I should not terminate from my job, but they did not give me a "God" reason. God wanted me to follow His plan because He had a better life for me. Can I be transparent, it was a struggle for me to make the decision, but I love God too much and I needed too much from Him not to come in compliance with His Word. He's all I have. My hope is in Him and my trust is in Him... He is the Bishop of my soul!

I need a God that can speak to me. Perhaps God has given you instructions for the next half of your life, but these instructions seem awkward, without rhyme, or reason, it is not within the range of normalcy – Remember, His instructions do not cater to rational or to man's way of thinking. But somewhere deep down in your Holy Ghost you know that you know that you know it is God speaking to you about you. No doubt, when the chapter of your life is in preliminary stages of change, God will give you a challenging word. This word will cause you to exercise immeasurable faith. When God speaks, He has already provided the resources and made the way. While walking on water – keep your eyes on Him… stay focused and see the "big picture."

My advice to you is, "obedience is better than sacrifice." How could God tell me to exit my job when I just received a promotion and how could He demand such a thing when He knew my situation? That is the reason, He demanded it because He knew my situation – He had something better for me, but I had to make room for Him to operate. I had to make room for Him to show me a miracle. And guess what? He did.

By submitting unto the instructions of God, I never regretted a moment of my life… God is trying to get you to step out of an old place and break away from old things. It may not be for you to come off your job like it was for me, but it could be something that you have been wrestling with for a long time. In this season, you will have to take a leap of faith, just do it! He is changing you, He is transitioning you, and He is propelling you to a new place. Old things cannot go with a new you. This is why I love the Prophet Isaiah. In Isaiah 43 – the Prophet vetoes the things that were and bring them into the "now." That is what God is doing with us now. He is commanding you to be broken to obedience in effort that prosperity will follow. I speak over your life power, authority, success, and long life in Jesus name.

KINGDOM ADVANCEMENT

The Kingdom of God is at hand! The government of the Lord is enhancing and increasing and it has no end. In fact, the Kingdom of God is within you. God's ruling and reigning power is in you. The Bible says that we have the keys to the kingdom of heaven. Mind you, God did not give us the keys to the church, but to the Kingdom. In the church everything belongs to you, but in the kingdom everything belongs to God.

These keys give you legal right to operate out of the authority of God and to make a transfer from heaven into the earth realm. "Our Father who art in heaven hallowed be thy name thy kingdom come..." So that which is in heaven, God has given you legal right to bring in to your life and into the lives of those who are connected to you. Therefore say, not out of the flesh, or your canal mind, but out of your spirit-man, "let the poor say I am rich, let the weak say I am strong, let the sick say I am healed, and let the captive say that I am delivered." The authority to "call the things that are not as though they were" operates in you.

When you have keys, you have influence and power. I possess three keys: 1) to my house 2) to my car, 3) to my church. I have a legal right to these three things/places. I have the authority to go and come as I please. God has given us the keys to the Kingdom of heaven. Therefore, I have power, through Jesus Christ to "bind and loose." According to Matthew 18:18 - "…whatsoever ye shall bind on earth shall be bound in heaven: and whatsoever ye shall loose on earth shall be loosed in heaven."

Through this scripture, I have undeniable power and authority! This power and authority that I have obtained from Jesus Christ is legal. Why, because I have a relationship with Him. I commune with Him, I walk with Him, and I "sup" with Him - I am in relationship with Him. And because He knows me and I know Him, He can trust me with His power and authority to be a blessing to His Kingdom. "Now unto Him that is able to do exceedingly and abundantly, above all that you ask or think according to the power (Kingdom of God) operating in you!"

For this reason, God the Father sent His Son Jesus to earth to destroy the works of darkness in your life. When you operate out of Kingdom authority, people will suggest that you are arrogant, but it is not that you are arrogant it is that you are confident. The bible states, "Be ye confident in this very thing, He who have begun a work in you..." Kingdom builders are confident people, they are royal priesthood people. Not only that, but they are a peculiar people. They operate out of a different vein from those of the world.

God has given you ruling authority that you can go on the enemy's territory and "take over!" Through this, God will begin to place His people in strategic geographical locations to bring change. Not for one moment should you think that you live in your community because you reside in your dream house, not for one moment should you think that you are employed with your present company because no one else was qualified, not for one moment should you think your business is located in a regal area or an urban area, but you are there because you have Kingdom authority to bring about change – change the existence of the people, the atmosphere, and the environment of those who need a relationship with

Christ and the change that will lose an anointing to make life easier for those who have a desire to connect with spiritual things. You have an anointing and authority to "make things better" you as a kingdom builder, have the authority to "take over!" Be blessed!

YOU ARE EPIC!

Immediately the Lord spoke to me of your uttermost concern... the Kingdom of God! The Lord is redefining your ministry and causing a global transfer of wealth and success. You are at the end of your third trimester and birthing a new measure of diplomatic sons and daughters. There has been much rebellion among the people, but God has given you a word as He gave Ezekiel... "Be not afraid neither be afraid of their words." God is spring boarding you into your "eon phase" of life... not only is this your season, but your "epic era."

You shall be a gatekeeper and trendsetter for this end time revival and many shall know you for the supernatural signs, wonders, and miracles. You shall be known as the Father of the Gospel and you shall be celebrated well. No longer shall the Ark of the Covenant be in Obedehim's house, but now it shall rest in your house... and the key of David shall rest upon your shoulder.

The Lord thy God shall legislate the laws of heaven and shall summons angels to war against every sabotaging spirit that would hinder you and your family. Your boundaries are shifting and your territories are enlarging – you shall call forth a holy assembly and the voice of God shall be in your Spirit – and you shall sound the alarm from the fruit of your lips. Pick up the new mantle that has been set before you Mighty Warrior – a mantle of many colors. As the Lord allowed Paul to go into a third heaven, so shall you! Right there... I just felt God change the function of your office, my God!!! As God redefines your ministry – Everyone will not have access to your anointing. It is imperative that you have a keen discernment of your nucleus. The bible declares in 1 Thessalonians 5:12.

THE GOD CONNECTION

"**A**nd we beseech you, brethren, to know them which labour among you..."

Connections! Who are you connected to? Who are you in relationship with? Do you know the spirit of those who have rule over you? Although this scripture relates to ministers as laborers, let's not reduce this writing to ministers. But let us relate this scripture to the Body of Christ in its entirety as referring to the relationships we have adopted and are connected to as labourers. When doing so, we must ask ourselves, "do we really those who labour among us?

Do we really know those who we have submitted our soul to? Are we connected to God-orchestrated relationship?" Also important to know is: 1) the purpose of the relationship/connections we are in; and 2) the season for the relationship/connections we are in. When the Lord is in the preparation stages of blessing an individual, He will always connect them to people who possess their investment.

These people are anointed to take us from "what shall be" into "that which shall become" – rather spiritually or naturally. These people come with a death certificate in one hand and a birth certificate in the other. Therefore; it is not important to be connected with several people during our spiritual formation, but be connected to the "God sent" person who is anointed for the appointed time; and the person who has the ability to bring us into our wealthy place. That is important! I feel an unction to tell you... "God is getting ready to send a "David Connection" that will bring you out of Lo-debar! Just as God used David to bring Mephibosheth from out of nothingness to the king's table, to palace floors; so shall He do for you (2 Samuel 9)!"

As we talk about connections, all relationships are not everlasting. Eighty-two percent of people who labour among us are only in our lives to make or receive a deposit. And when that deposit is made or received, the connections are released. Word of

Wisdom: Know the purpose for your connections and relationships. Also important, take on the spirit of Issachar and know the season of departure.

Let us not forget Abraham and Lot's connections. He brings Lot with him at the time of His departure into a new country (in Genesis 12), but soon departs from Lot (Genesis 13). "When Abram and Lot had pitched their tent unto the place of the altar between Bethel and Hai, the bible says the land was not able to bear them that they might dwell together; for their substance was great. And there was strife between the herdsmen of Abram's cattle and Lot's cattle..." Abraham knew that the season had come for departure. A time of release was at hand. Abram's purpose for carrying Lot was to make a deposit in him that would bring him to a wealthy place. But Abram used God's wisdom to know the season for this disconnection.

Subsequently, who you labour among is very essential as a Born Again Believer. God will send people who celebrate us for what He is doing in our lives at the present time. He will send people who will bless us and support us. These people never look for praise, never look for an allotment, or never look for a return... they know through revelation by the Spirit of the True and Living God that they have been assigned to our lives for a purpose. That purpose should only be to serve as a conduit to bring our destiny into existence and/or introduce us to something of value.

When my husband proposed to me 18 years ago, I went to my mentor and shared the good news about my "husband-to-be." In the conversation, I asked him if he thought my "husband-to-be" was the right man for me.

Strangely enough, he answered as such: "Is he a blessing or is he the wiles of the enemy?" When God makes a divine connection or a relationship is divinely orchestrated by God, we walk under the blessing of the Lord and not the curse of Satan. On the flip side of being in relationships... when Satan is trying to pull you out of the Spirit to curse you, he will assign the "wrong person" or cause you to connect to the wrong neighborhood, the wrong place of employment; the wrong relationship, the wrong investment, and, etc.

As a result, the spirit of deception will cause soul ties to take root. These soul ties are very hard to sever; over a period of time, we become complacent not being in the will of God. Even as I am speaking, there is someone reading this book that has connected to the wrong person, place, investment, and/or even made the wrong choice of worship. In this, the enemy has made you believe that you are "stuck" in a miserable situation for the rest of your life; I come, in the Name of Jesus, to let you know that Satan has lied to you! God is able and will deliver you from all your misfortunes, mistakes, shame, guilt, and afflictions!!! God is a deliverer!

I speak to your spirit now... What Satan tried to make a mess, God is overturning that mess, that captivity that yoke, that assignment, and that deception! The anointing is breaking up the "follo" ground! When life is always chaotic, full of disparities, and nothing seems to connect, take an assessment of our nucleus. Check your atmosphere. If you are in constant cycle, constant struggle, and constant battle – know those who you are connected to, know those who you are in relationship with, and know those you have rule over you. And most important, know those who labour among you!

When you have spiritually assessed your situation do not feel obligated to stay connected to or remain in a relationship that is not wholesome for your spiritual formation and/or your health. Often times breaking away may be painful, but remember God heals all wounds. Because your next level is important, it is necessary to only carry that which will be useful in you enhancing your growth in the things of God. I pray God give you "eagle eyes" to see in the spirit to those who labour among you that you shall know them by the spirit in which they operate!

I'm Blood washed, Prophetess Jacki London

TO THE INTERCESSORS

Those who can stand in the gap, as you go to a deeper dimension, such as intercessors, watchmen on the wall, sharpshooters in the spirit, and spiritual navy seals - God is changing the dimension of prayer. Intercessors do not "pray about" they "pray through." God is looking for those who are willing to stay on the altar until they "pray through." God has need of these types of intercessors because the demonic forces of darkness have intensified in the earth realm. Put on your weapons of war to loose global war faring angels, to build your altars!

In the day when you cry out from God's Kingdom, which has taken resident within you, The Lord thy God shall answer and make you bold with strength in your soul.

You will become a dangerous force to be reckoned with, a life changer, a history maker, a trendsetter, and an agent of change. In this season, you will serve as My battle axe and a dragon slayer.

I am giving you influence to build up kingdom and to tear down kingdoms, to build up nations and to tear down nations. You have the power and authority- the power of my might! Power to take over the atmosphere, the hemisphere, the stratosphere, and the spirit realm. Be bold as a lion, but meek as a lamb. My divine power will give you all things that pertain to life and my godliness. I have called you into glory and virtue.

Where are the intercessors for the Body of Believers? According to Ezekiel 22:30, there are none. Take very seriously the deplorable prophetic statement made to Israel through the prophet Ezekiel: "I sought for a man among them that should stand in the gap, but I found none." This concerns me! Ezekiel's inquiry prompts me to believe that he is still speaking to the 21st Century church. Where are the real men and women of God? What is the position of the ecumenical church? Is it just an envogue social gathering? Or is it the cosmos thing to do – attend church on Sunday morning and Wednesday evening? Or is it "flesh on parade?" Have we, as believers, put more emphasis on "how to get rich quick" than "how to live a consecrated and holy lifestyle?"

When we observe the prophetic voice of Ezekiel, we find that he is a prophet of a priestly family. When he was about 25 years old, he went under the regime of Nebuchadnezzar, the king of the Neo- Babylonian Empire. Ezekiel identifies himself as a priest. For historical context, he was the prophet that God allowed the tragedy of his wife's ("the desire of the eyes") death to be an example to Israel in preparation for the death of the city they loved. The prophet's contention was that Israel had caused much sin and guilt to the nation, but not one had done anything to bring a cleansing. He was distraught because of the prophets who testified of their love for God had become deceivers and devourers; also the priest who were teachers by office, had violated the law of God. They did not put a difference between the holy and profane, the clean and the unclean; they hid their eyes from God's Sabbaths and looked another way.

The people, who had power in their hand, abused it. There is none that appears as an intercessor for Israel. Sound familiar? When Paul dialogues with Ephesus church, I often wonder why the "office of the intercessor" was not a part of the five-fold ministry, being that the first century church was built on prayer. When you review the event on the Day of Pentecost, the Bible makes note that one hundred and twenty unified themselves and interceded that the promise would be fulfilled.

On that day, intercessory prayer brought forth the pivotal point of the operation that sanctioned and validated the apostolic church. God is the same today as He was yesterday. Direction is birthed through intercession, vision is birthed through intercession, and churches are birth through intercession.

When seven women would gather around my dining room table every Saturday at 12 noon for intercessory prayer (for three years), I had no idea the Lord was calling forth a holy assembly for the sake of birthing the Pillar of Fire Worship Center. To this date, intercession plays an integral part in our bible study, worship service, evangelism services, and even our region. The mantle of intercession has been laid down and God is waiting patiently to find an earthen vessel to impart His voice to bring dominion and kingdom on earth.

The bride of Christ must relinquish this mantle and take on the spirit of Issachar in effort to move in the time and season of God to release HIS judgment against the enemy. God wants a people who will not be ashamed or afraid to go to a realm in the spirit that will allow them to engage in warfare against the demonic activity and circumstances, a people who will not come under the subjection or align themselves with master spirits of the enemy.

There is an apostolic reformation in the earth to restore the church back to the Book of Acts. The power of the Rauch is calling all intercessors to sell out; to differentiate the holy and the profane, the clean and the unclean. The power of Rauch is seeking for those who refuse to hide their eyes from God's Sabbath and not look the other way. In essence what is God looking for? He is looking for a nation of people that will lay every weight aside and every sin that so easily beset them; a nation who will present their bodies as living sacrifices; a nation of people who refuses to take "shortcuts" to receive the mantle of an intercessor; a nation of people who will "sell out;" a nation of people who will lay on the threshing floor and become broken to submissiveness.

Who will stand in the gap? Where are the Prophetess Annas – the ones willing to pray until there is a birthing; the Simeons- the ones willing to pray until that which is in heaven will come in the earth; the Ezekiel's – the ones that will pray until the Shekinah Glory covers the city; the Peter's – the ones who will pray until heaven and earth have a spiritual collision? Is there one that can bring an ambassadorial, intercessory dimension in our midst that will blow a trumpet in the city to alert and awakened the church in effort to call us out of a state of dormancy and stagnation; to call us out of the state of tradition and religiosity?

There is a paradigm shift being released, not only in the atmosphere, but in your spirit. I am writing this book to you because God finds you trustworthy to flow in this anointing. He has chosen you from the foundation of the earth to pick up this "intercessory" mantle. There is a new authority that God has released in your spirit. This release is causing you to shift out of an old season of slothfulness, lack, poverty, and depression... there is a new state of dimension causing your ears to open to a new sound of revival.

There is a wave of a fresh move of God being released to you, new sight, new revelation, and a new dimension that will give you the power to reach that realm in the spirit to take power over sickness, to overtake and overturn the captivity of your children, loved ones, prayer partners, take power over a disturbed home, over a sick mind, over unemployment, over worry and anxiety, over sabotage and conspiracy, over fear, and witchcraft. No longer shall we pray the "wrong" prayer, but from this day forth the voice of God will be in the spirit of His people (those who are reading this book) to pray a prayer of "breakthrough" that will overturn the captivity of the church and bind the hand of the oppressor.

Church, when we get in the posture of the true intercessor, then shall we summons angels to marshal in heaven for us; when we posture ourselves in right position – then shall we have the dominion power to legislate the laws of heaven here on earth. Get ready, it's time for those who have suffered and died in the flesh and it's time for those who have turned off their flesh to hear the voice of God calling them in a deeper dimension of prayer and consecration. "Zion is calling you higher!" Wake up out of your sleep and stand in the gap – it's time for the real men and women of God to make the enemy the church's footstool. The Lord is a strong tower, the righteous run in and are safe! Be safe in Jesus name!

GOD IS A COVENANT KEEPER

God spoke to David through Nathan in 2 Samuel 7:3 – "Whatever you have in mind, go ahead and do it, for the Lord is with you!" David's zeal for the Lord is proven by his desire to build a temple to house the ark, however he was denied. Although denied, God made a promise to David that He would build Him a house. The covenant God made with David was that he would have a son that would succeed him and establish a kingdom and that this son would build the temple for the Ark of the Covenant to be housed.

This son, being named Solomon, would be established forever. Although this covenant was interrupted by the Babylonian exile, God kept his promise to David that his right to rule would remain in his dynasty. David did not mourn the loss of his privilege to build the temple, but embraced the promise and acknowledged God's authority to be God! (When our prayers are not answered in the order we have prayed, know that "everything is moving by the power of God.") The sovereign reign of Jesus Christ has the ability to transfer dominion power.

When I look at my children and grandchildren, I respect the fact that my children will, one day, be blessed by my prayers. Maybe that does not mean much to you, but I honor God for honoring and overshadowing my children with His glory due to my posture in Him. This is why I continue to keep a stance of victory, if not for me, let it be for my children. I feel the blood of Jesus flowing and covering our children right now! I feel angels encamping around and about them right now.

Every morning it is necessary that we release our children into the apostolic and prophet authority of God. This enables them to stand strong in the midst of diabolic spirits, thus causing demons to tremble at their presence; thus causing healing to take place in their schools and places of employment, thus causing what the devil wanted to do, he shall not be able to stand before them with evil.

As I was reading 2 Samuel 7, I experienced the awesomeness of God Almighty. I really felt the power of His Son, Jesus Christ! God is a promise keeper and to those who believe, that is who He is. God gets pleasure in their prosperity.

The historical context of this chapter is that David brings the Ark of the Covenant to Jerusalem. The ark was to be carried by the sons of Kohath and not by a cart or a vehicle. The sin was the touching of the ark by Uzzah and Ahio sons of Abinadab; it was not to be carried by anyone other person than the Levites as God had instructed. Not only did they transport it by a cart, they set the ark on a new cart. As Ahio was walking in front of it, David and the whole house of Israel were celebrating with all their might. To celebrate means to honor or praise publicly.

When they came to the threshing floor of Nacon; Uzzah reached out and took hold of the ark of God and the oxen stumbled. The Lord's anger burned against Uzzah because of his irreverent act, therefore God struck him down and he died there beside the ark of God. Obedience is better than sacrifice! David was angry because the Lord's wrath had broken out against

Uzzah and David became afraid of the Lord and said, "How can the ark of the Lord ever come to me?"

Because David felt unworthy, he put the Ark of the Covenant in Obed-Edom's house for three months and the Lord blessed him (Obed-Edom) and his household. I want to stop here to let you know that God is getting ready to bless you and your household. You may not deserve it and you may feel you are not worthy to receive what God is getting ready to do. There comes a time in our lives that we can no longer hinder the blessings of God entering into our lives... "You are blessed because God says you are blessed!"

Today is your day to receive the Ark of the Covenant in your house and it shall stay for a season. The ark stayed in Obed-Edom's house for three months – a season. This is the season for your prayers to be manifested, this is the season for your dreams to come to fruition, and this is the season for you to start dreaming and shouting again. It is time for you to feel joy and peace, again. This is the season of power and prosperity – a new season is coming your way!

As David got angry with the Lord and if we continue our spiritual formation, we too, will get angry with the Lord because we have fallen short. Through

104

this period, the enemy will want us to believe that we are not good enough, saved enough, and that we've been forgotten about. He will make us feel like its useless, it's over, and that nothing is working for me. He wants us to believe all sorts of negative impressions, but I come to tell you that the devil has lied to you!

On this day, the Ark of the Covenant is coming to your house. Yes, you've been disobedient, yes, you've sinned, and yes you've made excuses... so did David. He knew how the ark was to be transported from town to town, but he wanted to modernize or do it "a different way"... You know how we as Christians want to do it, "a new way, a better way, a different way, or a more convenient way." But if it is not "God's way" it is the wrong way and if it is not God way, it is disobedient. But look how God's grace covered David's disobedience after he begins to worship and make a sacrifice unto God.

When David returned home to bless his household and his wife, Michal got angry with his praise and accused him of disrobing himself in the sight of the slave girls. Oftentimes people don't understand your praise, but that is because they don't know where God has brought you from. They don't know what you've been through to get to this place, they don't realize you had to fight some demons to make it "here," and they don't understand it was time you couldn't even say "Jesus" more less tell your neighbor to say it!

See, David came from wearing sheepcote to wearing a priestly, royal robe that constituted him as being King over Israel. He felt he owed God praise – "a look back" praise. God had not only promoted him, but is now promising to bring promotion to a son that he does not even know. God, oh God! He's getting ready to do it for you; the Ark of the Covenant is coming to your house this day! And the blessings of the Lord maketh you rich and add no sorrows.

I prophesy to you and your children this day:

"I will take you from a wilderness place, in which you were following and living in a barren land; to being a ruler over much. I have been with you wherever you have gone, thus saith the Lord, God Almighty. I have cut off all your enemies this day from before you and now I will allow my greatness to flow out of you. I will provide a place in me for you and for your household, in which you will no longer be disturbed by the wickedness of evil. I will raise up your sons and daughters after my likeness and I will establish them and my love will never be taken from them because I have learned of your works unto me. Your home will forever house the Ark of the Covenant. I speak change in your family relations and in your household. The demon powers of hell shall be scattered and the power of the Holy Ghost shall rise in your house and all nations of people shall call you and your household blessed, thus saith the Lord!" These may seem as mere words to you, but flesh and blood did not reveal this to you; however it was God's spirit that has spoken this over your life. They are words of power and authority.

DOMINION POWER

According to Proverbs 18:21, it reads that out of my mouth I will declare, decree, and demand that there is miracle in my house. Although words are not visible, they have substance. They serve as symbols that bring life. God brought life to the universe from a dark place when He said, "Let there be light!" The universe was spoken out of the mind of God – it was spoken out of a dream. Words released into the atmosphere do not disappear and dissipate. Words are oxidized and they are "Zoë." They have life! They have no geographical limitations or demographic barriers.

Words have prophetic implication. They create a force that brings forth a manifestation of what you speak. They are suspended in the realm of the spirit awaiting the proper time and condition for the manifestation. Some things that have occurred in your life past or present have been created and released because you spoke it forth. You cannot afford to release capricious words out of your mouth because the spirit realm takes every word you speak as a command and mandate. The spirit realm does not discriminate between jokes, gestures, desires, orders, or a decree. Therefore, it is important to speak positive, life-changing words, and dominion over every situation that concerns you. Even in your daily dialogue.

The earth, hemisphere, and universe are waiting for you to give them instructions. The earth, though the spoken word, has to yield your increase. It waits in expectancy and anticipation for you to speak words of instruction in order to bring God's original intent back to the earth realm in effort that you may multiply, replenish, and subdue the earth.

It is important that you become aware of the fact that every word you speak is impregnated with power. Please condition yourself to choose your words correctly and use the correct combination of words. Why? The bible tells us, that "life and death lie in the power of the tongue." When you pray take authority and overcome everything that threatens your ascent (or "way up") into the realm of success and prosperity.

No longer do you as "spirit led" sons and daughters have to beg or cry for anything. You walk in the realm of dominion, authority and have a raw anointing from God that has the power to declare, decree, and demand a "thing" and "that thing" shall be established. In this dispensation of time, you have legal rights through Jesus Christ to legislate (make laws), institute (set in operation), confirm (formal approval), settle (to put in order), summons (send notice to appear at a certain place), and to authorize (justify). You have a kingly attributes as a believer (1 Peter 2:9). Therefore, you can pray dominion over your family, business, ministry, employment, and every realm of your life.

In 1 Samuel 17:46-51, David addresses His enemy with authority. He said, "This day the Lord will deliver you into my hand..." Guess what? Goliath was dead long before he was struck by the stone and beheaded by the sword. Before it happened – David spoke it. Isaiah 55:11 is one of my favorite scriptures, "My word will not return unto me void, but will accomplish that what I sent it to do!" "I speak dominion authority over every area of your life – that God is right now overturning your captivity and every hindering "thing" that is in your life.

I declare warfare against the thorn in your flesh and I release the anointing over your life that will dissipate every struggle, every spirit of lack, procrastination, sabotage, manipulation, and conspiracy. I pray that yokes of bondage will be destroyed, generational curses be broken, and generational blessings be released. I decree, declare, and demand that God Almighty will perfect that which concerns you in this season and you will no longer be called forsaken, but a city that is sought out!"

Not only are your "words" powerful, but so are your "thoughts." Do not underestimate the power of your thoughts. Proverbs 23:7 declares, "Whatsoever a man thinketh, so is he!" That's powerful... whatever your predominate focus is what you permit to exist in your life or is what you become. Many times, Christians focus on negativity and as a result we live in a cycle of negativity. It is important that we train our minds to think in the positive. In the book of Philippians, Paul says we need to "think on things that are lovely, whatsoever things that are of a good report; if there be any virtue, and if there be any praise, think on these things." (Philippians 4:8)

When we read Genesis 13:14-18, what was God teaching Abraham? First, He was teaching him to focus. "Lift up thine eyes, and look..." Focus feeds your faith or confirms your fears. Second, He was teaching him how to visualize. "for all the land which thou seest to thee will I give it." Thirdly and lastly, He was teaching him to have bigger thoughts. "Arise; walk through the land in the length of it and in the breadth of it..."

Don't focus on things or people smaller than what you are hoping for from God. Because with God, the "sky" isn't the limit! With God you can never think too big, too grand, or too great! According to Ephesians 3:20, God does "crazy big" stuff. You just have to think outside of the box! And when you think, think strategically. God will give you specific times lines, goals, objectives, and resources. He will even go so far as to show you who to incorporate in your vision and how to execute what you are thinking. If you connect with the wrong business partner, or negotiate with the incorrect mortgage company or financial institute in its inception period, you can literally "blow" the plan God has endorsed.

Be careful who you connect with, get in God's presence and seek His face for specifics. If you find it necessary; change your environment. Your environment impacts your attitude and your attitude forms and contributes to your way of thinking. Risk taking can sometimes be a factor. Ninety percent of my successes happened because I took a risk.

When the finances were not there, I purchased a home – I took a risk; when I stepped into pastoring and people were not there, I took a risk; when I had to decide rather to resign from my secular job and return to school, I took a risk. In order for something to live, something must die... You will have to take a risk! At one point in King David's life there was so much chaos – he dialogued with God and ask Him, "Must I pursue?" He knew there were risks involved when going on the enemies camp... but he took the risk and recovered not some, but all!

Success and prosperity hinges on what lies in your mind. Mark 9:23 says, "If thou canst believe, all things are possible to him that believeth." Think about it, God has given us a world of possibilities and they are waiting to be released into our future. God wants to bring the characteristics of heaven into your life. Focus and visualize on what God is saying in this season for you and yours. I know with assurance that the year 2014 is a year of "Apostolic Fulfillment and Birthing."

The Lord is taking space out of distance – the hour is now, the appointed time is now, and the set time is now. Think like an entrepreneur, think like you are the CEO, think about your next position, and think which community you would like to live in, "think on these things!" When life was at its worse, Paul told King Agrippa, "I had to think myself happy!" And as you think and as you pray, speak the word…"Now unto Him that is able to do exceedingly, abundantly, above all that we ask or think according to the power within us." And it is a "done deal!"

I speak over your life. In this hour, anything that would decoy or sabotage you from the assignment and purpose given to you; be disengaged by Jehovah Sabaoth. Any further impressions of the enemy that would come to your mind, I overthrow! Works of liars who have falsely accused you and tried to assassinate your character/integrity let them be renounced and denounced. Out of the prophetic oil that flows from within, I suffer not the spirit of evil doers, master spirits of witches, warlocks, and wizards to live in your presence.

The Lord, God shall draw out his sphere to bruise the head and cut the tongue of the enemy. Those who have caused your demise will be like withered grass and put to shame. I dismantle and cancel any satanic operations against you place the mandate that God has given you. Those who try to kill your dream, I prophesy... will die trying! And though many may question your readiness, I speak and declare that you are not out of your season, but you are moving according to Kairos. I superimpose every prophetic word and release an apostolic government into your life, in which signs and wonders will follow you this day. Be encouraged in Jesus!

WHAT GOD IS DOING IN THIS SEASON
IS MARVELOUS

The master plan that God has for you is unconditional. Your footsteps to this place in life have been ordered by the Lord. What an explosive time... life is now taking a road of its own through the Holy Spirit. God is beginning to do some things out of order and things that aren't in sequence. Things are getting ready to take an unexpected turn... He is turning things over and shaking bushes just for you, His beloved. Honestly speaking, it has nothing to do with you, but the people you will meet in the next six months. There is a testimony that God will allow to come forth out of your Spirit like rivers of living water. A testimony that will make a deposit in someone's life to assure them that, "Jesus is real!" This will be a testimony that will cause people to live and not die.

Through your trials and tribulation, God has given you the signet ring and a coat of many colors as a proven fact that heaven has documented. The Holy Spirit of God has validated you as a first class citizen in the category of "THESE ARE THEY!" The tribulations have been great, but you are an overcomer! The power of God is moving in your favor to bring forth a divine connection, a divine intervention, and divine favor.

"And ye shall be my people and I will be your God."

Now is the hour that bridges you to forgotten and unanswered prayers; prayers that you have stored in your secret closet and left on the shelf. Miraculous testimonies shall come forth. The mighty hand of God reaches on those dusted shelves bringing to pass those utterances that seemed impossible. The atmosphere has been made conducive to receive the release from the spirit realm to the earth realm.

God is transferring His power from the throne room to you in effort that it may empower and impact you to operate out of a higher level. Also, to receive the manifestation and demonstration of the unfolding mystery that your deepest desires are hinged upon. He gets the glory; Go tell someone else of His goodness and His mercy, how He brought you out.

It is good that you are in this place! This place is a place of brokenness. This place is a place of being "sold out," a place where He has pitched a tent for you and built an ark. Sojourn in this place. This place is a place of "if I perish, let me perish, but I'm going to see the King! I feel a "nevertheless" anointing coming upon somebody who is reading this book. You know why I feel a "nevertheless" anointing? Well let me tell you; somebody who has been going through hell for the last ten years, is getting a "breakthrough," somebody who had to live with demons for the most part of their life is getting a "breakthrough," somebody who had been "dogged" out and don't know what to do, is getting a "breakthrough." Because when "nevertheless" hit's the atmosphere, you can't help, but to break free – it's the anointing that destroys the yoke!

The anointing is operating in the atmosphere. Excuse me, I'm receiving a fax from God, it says… "Quickly, submerge yourself under Rauch and do not operate outside the elements of the Holy Spirit." When the anointing hits the atmosphere it comes to take resident in two ways: 1) to gird you up; and 2) to speak!

As you read, the anointing is speaking to your spirit – I'm hearing, "delayed don't mean denied, you are in sync with Me, this is your appointed time."

Can I tell you what the anointing is saying? The anointing is saying "this is your third day, it is finished, and all your prayers are being answered!" That is what the anointing is saying. Out of your brokenness God will require of you to do things you've never done before to get what you've never had. Must I say this dispensation of your life... the rules change. God will require, not faith of a grain of a mustard seed, but immeasurable faith. The Bible says in Luke 12:48 that, "For unto whomsoever much is given, of him shall be much required..."

Your faith is being mandated. Reason being is because you never thought this could happen for you – you never knew God this way! Therefore you must rise up and receive in your spirit, "Your eyes have not seen, your ears have not heard, nor has it entered into the heart of man what God has prepared for you!" Listen, that is not when you get to heaven, this is now! It is taking immeasurable faith to grab what God is doing in the earth realm; the strangeness of God is being exposed to those who can believe immeasurably.

God is establishing a covenant in you, everything you set out to do – the Holy Spirit is going to back you in power… "Behold, the days come, saith the Lord, that I will make a new covenant with the house of Israel, and with the house of Judah: Not according to the covenant that I made with their fathers in the day that I took them by the hand to bring them out of the land of Egypt, which my covenant they brake, although I was an husband unto them, saith the Lord, But this shall be the covenant, that I will make with the house of Israel, after those days saith the lord, I will put my law in their inward parts and write it in their hearts: and will be their God, and they shall be my people." Praise our God that sounds like good news… it is good news!

Lastly, obey God rather than man. God has the power to exalt you. Promotion does not come from the north, south, east, or west; it comes from God. Why do I interject this statement because the enemy will try to make deals and transactions with you to abort your miracles. In this hour, he will try to deceive you through people that are assigned to bring you under the control of witchcraft (rebelliousness) – to pull you out of the spirit realm. Their way will look right and good, but they won't look "God." The Bible says, "There is a way unto man that seems right, but the end shall bring forth death." Satan will try to influence you to operate in the realm of sense and knowledge, but not so! This is a God "thing," this is God's way... when the enemy comes in like a flood; let the purpose of God be released out of your mouth. God has exalted you to a place in Him in a double fold measure – to be a blessing and to receive a blessing.

Don't let the trickery of the enemy move you out of position. "My sheep know my voice and a stranger's voice they shall not hear." The Lord knoweth how to deliver the Godly out of temptations and to reserve the unjust unto the Day of Judgment to be punished. Remember, what you have gone through and what you are getting ready to be blessed with is not about you, but it is to bring glory to God's name that others may see Him in an exalted position.

When you lift up the name of Jesus somebody will be delivered and saved. This is why the enemy would want to silence you; this is why the enemy would want you to believe He is the exalted one. Now, let us not forget, the enemy does not come in a red suit with horns and a pitchfork. He operates through someone who knows your weakness and then presents an opportunity to expound in that area. Stay focused! What God is doing in you, strangely enough, is not about you, but About His glory. That is why it is important that I say to you, "guard your spirit and protect your anointing!!" So that you can forever give God praise and glory for His wondrous works. If you do these things, the master plan of God will never cease to operate in your life, it will unfold! The unanswered and forgotten prayers will manifest and there will be a demonstration of the power of the Holy Ghost in your life. Continue fighting the good fight of faith, immeasurable faith – it is your moment to come forth in the things of God. Come forth in the God given vision and make the dream a reality!

"Lift up your heads all ye gates... who is the King of Glory?"

Solomon coined the book Ecclesiastes by saying, "Vanity of vanities, all is vanity!" Call me not Solomon (peaceable) because sin has brought me to this place – call me Marah (great bitterness). In spite of the name changing and the sins committed, to my surprise, he calls himself "the preacher." I wonder if the reason is being contributed to his God consciousness leading him to know that God beginning a work in him does not disregard the intimate of his character. Or is it because he has been made in the image of God? Or could it be he now understands that when God called him from the foundation of the earth into destiny and purpose that could never be reversed?

When God births us and processes us through the Spirit, no demon in hell, no witch on earth, no diabolic activity can reverse our sonship in Jesus Christ. I feel right here in the middle of this sentence, that it is important for you to know this... some of us think that what we did last night negates the call of God in our lives, some think that what we didn't do last night nullifies the call of God in our lives. THE DEVIL IS A LIAR!

You are who you are because God said so and God never changes! We may go into isolation for a period of time, we may struggle for a period of time, we may face some midnights for a period of time, we may sit by the brook of Serith for a period of time, or be on the back side of the mountain, but through it all, we are who God called us to be. He is the same today, as He was yesterday. He is not a "respecter of person."

The theme I would like to address for this Good Morning, Holy Spirit is, "You can't unchange what God has changed", based on Ecclesiastes 3:14. We live in a world of changes, several events at a time. The conditions of human life are vastly different from one another – there is always a constant ebbing and flowing. In our spiritual formation we go from one extreme to another, but one thing you can be sure of is that the open hand of God is in all these changes. Through these changes, God is doing the unexpected, the supernatural, and the dominion. We may not understand "the change," but all changes in your life are dominated by the power of the Holy Ghost. The scripture that comes to my thinking is "all things work together for the good..." Romans 8:28.

The change many be inconvenient, adverse, or seem as though it is an assignment sent by Satan. But thank God for being able to intercept and turn the bad into good. Please take note that when the change brings us to a hard place in our lives and we can't "roll the stone away" or it seems as though we have been forgotten about, discontinue asking God – "What sin have I committed to cause such desolation and lament?"

It is not about what you have done - it is about what and where God is trying to take you. Through this transitional period, there are three focal points: 1) God is creating a new thing in our lives; 2) He is bringing us into a new chapter of living; and 3) He is causing our existence to change. He realizes that where we were, is too small for us to operate in Him and He operate through us. Therefore, He feels it is imperative that He ushers us into a place where our spiritual "gift (not talent) has made room for us." These pivotal moments can become fierce, but through the process of it all – we must remember there is no deficiency in what God does and He does operate in the unnecessary. When you are confronted with change, God feels it necessary to bring change in your life to transfer wealth and/or power.

Also, it is equally important that during this time we acknowledge His character in three ways: 1) His steadiness; 2) His grace which is all sufficient; and 3) His government of authority over our lives. These are agents who serve as under-girding strengths that allow us to go from one level to the next and one dimension to the next. His strength causes us to be "clothed in our right mind" without the assignment of the underworld attacks becoming effective as tools of abortion used against our next dimension of destiny.

Because we can only see the middle of God's works when we are in the cusp of a change, it is important that we judge nothing before its time. When we don't understand the move of God in our lives, we have to pray, stand back and "leave it alone!" Don't speak against your new place of residency in God and do not speak against this "extraordinary thing" God is doing in your life. Your colleagues, family members, friends, and prayer partners will question the events in your life that have brought about change. Especially when they cannot compartmentalize them, or when they see you less than perfect, or not in a position to receive a blessing. God is so awesome and the phenomenon that operates behind the scene cannot be questioned because He is God all by Himself. Thank God, He doesn't need any help. All I know is He reigns on the just, as well as the unjust. His reigning power over our lives validates and sanctions that "you cannot curse who God has called blessed."

God blessed Solomon with a dynasty promised to him through his father's righteousness. This lifestyle once made him happy, but there came a change in his life that caused him to realize that what was once most important to him had been reduced to becoming "vanity and vexation of the spirit." In a matter of seconds our lives can change, our circumstance can change, and we can change. Some of these changes are uncomfortable, some are mystical, and some are fierce. Whichever fit the description of your change, stay focused on the purpose of change and who brought about the change, which is God Almighty. Almighty means "without contenders." No matter how fierce and wicked Satan may appear to hinder what God is doing in your life, he cannot defeat God. In God's time and His way – He will fulfill His promises in reference to your transition and accomplish His sovereign purpose in your life.

Although everything around you can change: your address, your business, your marriage, your zip code, and your phone number, but who God called you to be – never changes. Your purpose and who God called you to be will never change. Solomon's name changed, his socioeconomic status changed, his nucleus changed, and his view on life changed, but who God called him to be from the foundation of the earth and from Bathsheba's womb, that never changed.

In spite of the vanity, the women, the mistakes, his lifestyle, and even in the midst of his depression and struggles, he still knew deep down that he was "the preacher" God called him to be. You, too, are fearfully and wonderfully made; you too, are a prophet from your mother's womb; you too, are blessed and highly favored; you too, are the head and not the tail; you too, are high and lifted up in the spirit; you too, are no longer a servant of God, but a friend of God... it's your era of power and prosperity, it's your moment.

God is all-powerful. No counter moves of the devil and no matter how strong the devil thinks he is, can frustrate the righteous purposes of God. The devil can't unchange what God has changed.

CONCLUSION OF THE MATTER

I n my closing, I hope I have encouraged you – it is my effort and earnest prayer that God is perfecting your life. I once remember sitting in the pews of my family church, as a child, I'll never forget, when one of my spiritual Mothers, jumped up with great enthusiasm walking down the middle aisle saying, "While you are trying to figure it out, God already done worked it out!" That cliché has always attached itself to my spirit, but more so as I was reading Mark 16:1-4. "And when the Sabbath was past, Mary Magdalene and Mary the mother of James and Salome, had brought sweet spices, that they might come and anoint Him (v.2) And very early in the morning the first day of the week, they came unto the sepulcher at the rising of the sun. (v.3) and they said among themselves, who shall roll us away the stone from the door of the sepulcher? (v.4) and when they looked, they saw that the stone was rolled away: for it was very great." While you are trying to figure it out, God already done worked it out!

Can you imagine how Mary must have felt eye witnessing the most hideous death of all mankind – this death being the death of her son, our Lord and Savior Jesus Christ? Even though she had witnessed his death and it seemed like a "sealed deal" it was her greatest desire to go and anoint him, as a Jewish custom, for the last time. She invited Mary Magdalene and Salome to walk with her down that long road where her son lay. Can you imagine the obstacles, adversities, and disappointments they encountered in reference to, as they walked?

I can hear the complaints now from Mary Magdalene and Salome how tired they were, how long the road was, and how hungry they were… all kinds of complaints, not to mention the spectators alongside the road that called her foolish saying, "Forget it, He's dead…never to rise again, you must be crazy, nothing like this has ever been done, it's a "sealed deal!" But Mary kept walking because she had an invincible determination to see her son "one more time." When you have an invincible determination – it's not good to take everybody with you.

It's not good to tell everybody what you and God talked about- because while you are walking out the plan of God you have some people who are not anointed to see down that long road. You have people who are not equipped to go where you are going; you have some in your nucleus that don't believe and operate on the faith level you operate out of. They will start out with you, but when the going gets rough and the times get tough those who are not anointed for the job won't last and those who are not anointed for the mission will start complaining and falling off to the wayside. As much as we love our friends and family we must realize that everybody can't handle where God is taking us. It hurts, but "so-be-it" and this is when we have to reach down in our Holy Ghost and say, "If I have to go by myself, I'll go by myself!" That's what you call invincible determination.

While Mary was walking down that long road she had begun to realize that the stone that sealed her son's sepulcher was inhuman to move because of weight. Not only inhuman to move, but against the law to move! So the odds were against her. Is this how it seems with the struggle you are facing today – the odds are against you, it's inhumanly possible to resolve, it's too heavy, to burdensome, and to weighty to move?

Does it seem like it is a "sealed deal?" The stone that sat at the entry way of Jesus' sepulcher was also sealed... But Mary's invincible determination caused heaven to shake, the angels to remove their gold studded crowns, and lay their harps on Calvary's shelf to go move that stone which was sealed at the entry way of the sepulcher where Jesus lay.

Have you been trying to figure out a survival mechanism through this economic crisis, how will you survive the "downsizing of your company, what about "Little Johnny" who is faced with a prison sentence, what about the daughter who has serious issues, don't forget the unjust education system that is trying to label your child negatively, the marriage you are tired of interceding for, the business that is plummeting, the depression, the cancer, HIV, sickness, loneliness, suffering, and you know the list goes on and on. But God!

When Mary got to the sepulcher, that which she had been worried about, had been taken care of in supernatural way! The Bible says, "The stone had been rolled away!" What an awesome God, we serve! Not only taken care of, but God went beyond what she wanted done. Sounds like a "now unto Him who is able to do exceedingly, abundantly, above all that we ask or think according to the power operating in us!" God will do more than you ask Him.

Sometimes, I don't believe God shares with us exactly what He is going to do because our eyes and our ears are not good enough to see or hear His next move for our lives. We may not believe – it may sound too "over the top." So I say unto you my brother and my sister… "The stone has already been rolled away!" So, this brings me back to what I heard over forty years ago from the Mother in my old church, as she walked down the aisle... "While you are trying to figure it out, God already done worked it out!" He is the risen Lord and Savior. He rose with all power! The Roman soldiers thought it was a "sealed deal," but we know that it is a "done deal" that we have the keys to the kingdom and we have authority to "bind and loose."

May God yoke you under His anointing and bring you under the captivity of His Holy Spirit, that His will shall continuously be operative in your life!

Good
MORNING
HOLY SPIRIT

JACKI LONDON

ABOUT THE AUTHOR

Jacki London

London is a Born-Again Believer and a Kingdom Builder. She was born to SFC Foster and Lillian Barfield in Colorado Springs, Colorado. She is also the founder and Pastor of Fire Worship Center in Warsaw, NC. She currently lives in New Bern, NC

She holds an Associate Degree in Psychology from Craven Community College, Bachelor of Arts Degree in Religion, and a Masters and Doctorate in Theology from North Carolina College of Theology.

Dr. London has 2 daughters; deShauna and Passion; six lovely grandchildren, who she says are the "apple of her eye": Lillian O'brien, deShon Montreal, Vinson Elijah, Shaakira Caleb, Kahlil, and Makalia Kodee.

Her hobbies are writing, abstracting painting, interior decorating, entertaining, listening to music, and teaching.

Is there a book inside of you? Ever wanted to self publish but didn't know how? Concerned about the financial part of self publishing? Relax. Take a deep breath. We can help!

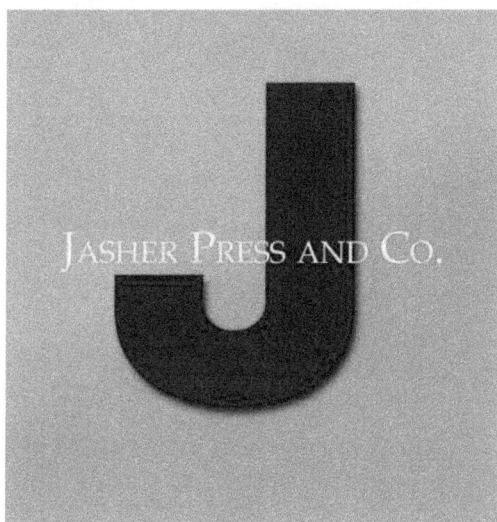

JASHER PRESS AND CO.

Finally! An affordable Self Publishing company for all of your Self Publishing needs. We have the right services, with the right prices with the right quality. So, what are you waiting for?

Unpack those dreams, break out that pen, your dreams of getting published may not be so far off after all!

Jasher Press & Co. is here to provide you with Consulting, Book Formatting, Cover Designs, editing services but most importantly inspiration to bring your dreams to past.

And this whole process can be done in less than 90 days! You thought about it, you talked about it but now is the time!